Fire

Fire

POEMS BY

Wesley McNair

DAVID R. GODINE · *Publisher*

BOSTON

First published in 2002 by
David R. Godine · *Publisher*
Post Office Box 450
Jaffrey, New Hampshire 03452
www.godine.com

LIBRARY OF CONGRESS

CATALOGING-IN-PUBLICATION DATA

McNair, Wesley.

Fire / poems by Wesley McNair

p. cm.

ISBN 1-56792-160-4 (softcover : alk. paper)

1. McNair, Wesley.

2. Poets, American—20th century—Biography.

3. Poetry—Authorship. I. Title

PS3563.C388 Z466 2001

811'.54—dc21   00-061045

FIRST EDITION
Printed in the United States of America

for Diane
and for Ruth

ACKNOWLEDGMENTS

Thanks to the following magazines in which poems of this collection have appeared:

The Alaska Review: "Sleep";

Del Sol Review: "Home," "The Invention of the Present";

The Kenyon Review: "Driving North in Winter," "Town Limits";

MARGIE: The American Journal of Poetry: "Voiceless," "When My Mother Called About the Fire";

Mid-American Review: "An Executive's Afterlife," "Smoking";

Ploughshares: "History of Talking on the Phone," "The Rules of the New Car";

Poetry: "Massive," "What Became";

Poetry Northwest: "Charles by Accident," "Goodbye to the Old Life," "How I Became a Poet," "My Stepfather's Hands," "Watch";

The Sewanee Review: "Shovels," "The Good-Boy Suit," "The Visitors";

Slate: "Speech";

The Southern Review: "My Mother Falling Asleep";

Virginia Quarterly Review: "The One I Think of Now," "What They Are";

Words & Images: "How She Told Him."

"Driving North in Winter," "Shovels," "The Unspoken," and "What They Are" were reprinted in *Contemporary Poetry in New England*.

"Goodbye to the Old Life," "Massive," and "Town Limits" appeared online on *Poetry Daily*; "What Became" was a featured poem on *Poetry* online.

Special thanks to Malcolm Cochran, Ellen Cooney, Daniel Gunn, Donald Hall, Peter Harris, Robert Kimber, Diane McNair, Shanna McNair, Patricia O'Donnell, Mike Pride, and Bill Roorbach.

Contents

HOME

Speech

How I Became a Poet

"Wanted" was the word I chose
  for him at age eight, drawing the face
  of a bad guy with comic-book whiskers
  then showing it to my mother. This was how,

  after my father left us, I made her smile
  at the same time I told her I missed him,
  and how I managed to keep him close by
  in that house of perpetual anger,

  becoming his accuser and his devoted
  accomplice. I learned by writing
  to negotiate between what I had,
  and that more distant thing I dreamed of.

How She Told Him

It was such an exuberant moment, up late
with friends and all of them laughing
over some harmless joke about what
the two of them do in bed, and she blushing,
blushing, at her age. Not even she
knows why, or why, a few nights later,
pulling the bedspread over her daughter
to kiss her goodnight, she thinks
of her own waiting lips and the covers
settling around her thighs. One afternoon
she's holding a towel after the shower
and sees a naked stranger drying herself
off through the mist on the mirror
and wants only to know her, to be her.
How can she tell him the whole thing started
in a confusion and sorrow that had nothing,
really, to do with him or another man,
like the wrong turn she takes making her
a full hour late and him begin to shout at her
and her to shout back without thinking
what she is saying until she has told him.

The Unspoken

Was there a funeral for him, the husband
who took his own life? If so,
it was unannounced, as he himself
had been, following the river bank
with his rifle and coming out
of the woods behind the town office
where she worked alone, that determined
she would never leave him, though she tried
one last time, crouching under the desk.
Filling the church to pay their last respects
to her, none of them thought to ask
about him, yet as they rose to speak,
he was the one they couldn't quite
find the words for. "A tragedy,"
said the neighbor who went into the barn
to put out the flames, not guessing
the husband had set fire to the house, too,
and was dead inside it. "This brave woman,"
said her confidante, meaning the alien
anger the wife could never escape.
"Her loving spirit," said the sister,
who understood that when the wife laughed
and fussed over him in the general store
or at the town meeting, it was not love but fear.

My Mother Falling Asleep

When my mother was eighteen,
she escaped from that tyrant,
her mother, and the brothers
she had to raise, ending up
five years later with a husband
who'd left her and my two brothers
and me. Was this when she began
to turn against her body,
denying it in the end
every pleasure? Angry with us,
she was angrier at herself,
staying up all night long
to sew the clothes she took in,
her mother on her mind.
Sleep was for people who had
nothing better to do, she said.
Were we on her mind too, then
and later, the sons she left behind
as her hands became intimate
with work in the small light
of her machine? Late in her life,
when work became her only true
friend and she gave up
regular meals, she dragged her body,
which no longer knew what
time it was, to the garden
to pick green beans or tomatoes

in the middle of the night.
Sitting to talk during the day,
she would clasp her arms together
and lean forward, closing
her eyes, until you were looking
at the crown of her old, crazed head.
I think of my mother falling asleep
in those moments, free of the self–
destruction and guilts she never
spoke about or found the words for.
I see her holding her body,
or it holding her, bringing her
slowly down into its folded arms.

Sleep

The young dog would like to know
why we sit so long in one place
intent on a box that makes the same
noises and has no smell whatever.
Get out! Get out! we tell him
when he asks us by licking the back
of our hand, which has small hairs,
almost like his. Other times he finds us
motionless with papers in our lap,
or at a desk looking into a humming
square of light. Soon the dog understands
we are not looking, exactly, but sleeping
with our eyes open, then goes to sleep
himself. Is it us he cries out to,
moving his legs somewhere beyond
the rooms where we spend our lives?
We don't think to ask, upset
as we are in the end with the dog,
who has begun throwing the old,
shabby coat of himself down on every
floor or rug in the apartment, sleep,
we say, all that damn dog does is sleep.

My Stepfather's Hands

I had never seen hands like that, with blunt
fingers that made their pink nails seem
almost delicate. He walked doubling them
into fists because, he said, this made people
take him seriously. My brothers and I
tried it too, but only felt more than ever
like the kids we were. When I watched him
tilt a spike against the upright stud I pressed
to the floor of the new goat shed and drive it
in with three strokes, my own hand twitched.
"TNT," my stepfather declared, "T'ain't
Nothin' To It," then poked the hammer
into my ribs. "Now you do it." I found reasons
for saying it to my brothers: "TNT."
One day after he unloaded the goats
from his pick-up, he cut the testicles off
the billygoat and tethered him with a stripe
of blood on his white fur. "He don't even
feel it," he said, wiping his knife-blade
on his pants and folding it back into its case
with his broad thumb. For the first time
I doubted what he told me, feeling
something like fear on each visit to the shed
where I listened to the goat's soft bleating
and stared into the slits at the center
of his yellow eyes. Gradually, when anger
overtook my stepfather, we came to fear

his hands, though on that day the baseball
from the game we played rolled toward him
working on the junk rototiller, his fist
was closed around a wrench. He stood,
reached down for the ball, and threw it,
to our shock, with no aim or control whatever,
just like a girl. Nobody turned to fetch it
where it fell after its wild arc, then
the three of us went at once, anxious
to pretend nothing had changed, in spite of all
we had learned my stepfather's hands couldn't do.

Voiceless

The swelling
that starts under the eye
of the mother rising
for third shift, then
turns into a welt.

The slow steps
of the ill man's hand
up the tenement
banister, skin
and knucklebone.

The silence of cats
watching the old woman
in a bathrobe explain to them
how everyone loved her
in the red dress.

The still chest of the wife
who has learned
not to have feelings
so her vigilant husband
will not know them.

The bowed head
of the boy set apart
from the others
in his chair
as if in prayer.

The face nobody sees
on the glass door
of the cooler, not even
the one who opens it to stock
cases, night after night.

Speech

All along, he wants us to know,
the simple solution he offers
has been right there, obvious

as his open palm. No wonder
he seems a little angry with us,
who have spent our time shrugging

our shoulders and teetering our right
hands back and forth, while he's
found this truth that makes right

and wrong perfectly divisible.
Does our doubt return
because of the loneliness

we sense in him, forming precise
compartments with his hands
at the lectern inside his small

beam of light? Or is it the absence
in his speech of an expression for two
things at once no language

seems complete without: *mas o menos*,
comme ci, comme ça, or that
stubborn, beautiful word *though*.

History of Talking on the Phone

Once the phone, called the "telephone,"
was a voice one heard by pressing
what looked like a stethoscope
to one's ear, answering by shouting
at a device on the wall.

This was before talking on the phone
was invented — a more intimate exchange
using a receiver that allowed one to speak
to the voice while holding it in the hand.

Everyone held it and spoke to it.

In stereoscope movies of the period, starlets
lounged on beds talking on the phone
as they stroked its long cord. Men in high-rise
offices commanded, "Put her through!"

or sat in bedrooms on a split screen
talking on phones that matched their pajamas.

In the small towns of America, the tender gesture
of hunching one shoulder to talk on the phone
became popular with housewives washing dishes

and men in the workplace, whose big shoulders
balancing the voice as they smiled and talked to it

while turning the pages of a parts catalogue
or toweling grease from their hands

made a poignant moment
in the history of talking on the phone.

In the cities, meanwhile, where phones
had begun to resemble miniature
p.c. keyboards, so square and flat
not even teenagers practicing on private lines
in their rooms could balance them,

talking on the phone rapidly advanced
to contacting someone on the phone,
or explaining what one wanted into a machine.

The voice, now a filed message,
was what one listened to all alone,

like the starlet in the movie
coming home all smiles after a week away
to the ominous dark of her apartment
and releasing voices

until she gets to the one
she can hardly believe and plays it

over and over, unable to stop crying.

When My Mother Called About the Fire

After the pump broke and she began
to use drip pans under the eaves
to water her flowering plants
and mosquitoes laid eggs in the drip pans,
she poured the water carefully, one
large corner to each small mouth until
there were dozens of plastic milk jugs
lined up in front of the house, then
capped them to kill the mosquitoes,
inventing in this way her new weekly
system of watering everything
in her overgrown nursery, the business
which, after my stepfather's death, existed
more and more in her mind where no one
could dislodge it, though we gently
tried, knowing her anger, knowing
in the end she would go right on
calling us about her workers who were like
family, or the boy she hired just
like her youngest son, putting it all
together at last with words, one half-asleep
sentence leading to the next like a runner
from an ivy or spider plant until
the whole conversation itself was overgrown,
so how were we to know this phone call

was different — the same urgency,
the same combination of all that was gone
and my mother determined she was the only
one who knew how to find it, as if
she were walking bent over down
the long path through her living room
and looking into the piles of newspapers
and clothes and half-used bags
of fertilizer and seeds — except this time
she could find nothing at all because
there were no newspapers or clothes
or bags of seeds or milk jugs,
and in spite of these words, this overgrown
thing she was putting together sentence
by sentence against her pain and loneliness
and everlasting death, everything was lost.

Afterlives

Massive

They never guessed
the dead man had something
so large as that
in him, yet each day

walking past their doors
down the long, fluorescent
hall toward his, he had been
carrying this

crisis about to happen,
this statement so massive
that making it
took everything he had.

All morning they gathered
outside the identical
hums of their offices,
uncertain what it meant

that he of all people,
the one they hardly knew
with the small, benign wave,
had caused the absence

they felt now in every memo,
policy, and deadline,
had gone and left
behind something so big.

Watch

Do you remember the teachers who refused
to accept the papers we passed in late?
Their classes ended with bells that rang
over and over until we couldn't hear them

because they were inside us. We were prepared
then for our Christmas watch, whose name
came from what grown-ups did with theirs,
checking them to determine how much longer

they had for one thing before they started
the next. How soon we learned to translate
its tiny code of angles into days, then years
of work, weeks off, and mortgage payments,

not realizing at first that the watch we wore
was watching us back, like a small,
unblinking eye, except it didn't really
care if it saw us or not, mechanical and dead

as it was. Nobody could teach us that all
that time, there was this delicate ticking
on the other side of our wrists, mysterious
in its origin, different for each of us, and alive.

The Invention of the Present

Encounter groups about the present sprang up
even in rural areas. People learned
to laugh together and let go
of empty relationships. Everybody held hands.

In religious shows on TV fat women
with rouge like bruises on their cheeks
and men with silver wigs who looked dead
sang never mind about yesterday,

Jesus loves you as you are. Operators are standing by
scrolled left to right under their feet.
On TV someone was always standing by
or shooting somebody or being shot

or telling jokes or saying don't delay
and be sure to act now. For suddenly,
it seemed to be all the present all the time.
Yet not even the present just happened

without the contributions of a number
of pioneers: Cher, for instance,
who experimented with gels and plastic surgery
to develop a face impervious to change,

the journalist who brought history into the present
by discovering that a bill signed
in Washington or a good day on Wall Street
were actually "historic moments,"

the manufacturers of automobiles
that made the future as near
as the neighborhood showroom.
For lacking them — and the creators

of multi-tasking and e-mail,
and the first voyagers into cyberspace,
bringing to that starless darkness
web-sites, on all the time at the same time —

we would never have known
that the whole idea of the past
could become a thing of the past;
we would never have had, in short, today.

What Became

What became of the dear
strands of hair pressed
against the perspiration
of your lover's brow
after lovemaking as you gazed
into the world of those eyes,
now only yours?

What became of any afternoon
that was so vivid you forgot
the present was up to its old
trick of pretending
it would be there
always?

What became of the one
who believed so deeply
in this moment he memorized
everything in it and left
it for you?

The Rules of the New Car

After I got married and became
the stepfather of two children, just before
we had two more, I bought it, the bright
blue sorrowful car that slowly turned
to scratches and the flat black spots
of gum in the seats and stains impossible
to remove from the floor mats. Never again,
I said as our kids, four of them by now,
climbed into the new car. This time,
there will be rules. The first to go
was the rule I made for myself about
cleaning it once a week, though why,
I shouted at the kids in the rearview mirror,
should I have to clean it if they would just
remember to fold their hands. Three years
later, it was the same car I had before,
except for the dent my wife put in the grille
when, ignoring the regulation about snacks,
she reached for a bag of chips on her way
home from work and hit a tow truck. Oh,
the ache I felt for the broken rules,
and the beautiful car that had been lost,
and the car that we now had, on soft
shocks in the driveway, still unpaid for.
Then one day, for no particular reason except
that the car was loaded down with wood
for the fireplace at my in-laws' camp

and groceries and sheets and clothes
for the week, my wife in the passenger seat,
the dog lightly panting beside the kids in the back,
all innocent anticipation, waiting for me
to join them, I opened the door to my life.

Goodbye to the Old Life

Goodbye to the old life,
to the sadness of rooms
where my family slept as I sat

late at night on my island
of light among papers.
Goodbye to the papers

and to the school for the rich
where I drove them, dressed up
in a tie to declare who I was.

Goodbye to all the ties
and to the life I lost
by declaring, and a fond goodbye

to the two junk cars that lurched
and banged through the campus
making sure I would never fit in.

Goodbye to the finest campus
money could buy, and one
final goodbye to the paycheck

that was always gone
before I got it home.
Farewell to the home,

and a heartfelt goodbye
to all the tenants who rented
the upstairs apartment,

particularly Mrs. Doucette,
whose washer overflowed
down the walls of our bathroom

every other week, and Mr. Green,
determined in spite of the evidence
to learn the electric guitar.

And to you there, the young man
on the roof turning the antenna
and trying not to look down

on how far love has taken you,
and to the faithful wife
in the downstairs window

shouting, "That's as good
as we're going to get it,"
and to the four hopeful children

staying with the whole program
despite the rolling picture
and the snow — goodbye,

wealth and joy to us all
in the new life, goodbye!

The One I Think of Now

At the end of my stepfather's life
when his anger was gone,
and the saplings of his failed
nursery had grown into trees,
my newly feminist mother had him
in the kitchen to pay for all
those years he only did the carving.
"You know where that is,"
she would say as he looked
for a knife to cut the cheese
and a tray to serve it with,
his apron wide as a dress
above his workboots, confused
as a girl. He is the one I think of now,
lifting the tray for my family,
the guests, until at last he comes
to me. And I, no less confused,
look down from his hurt eyes as if
there were nothing between us
except an arrangement of cheese,
and not this bafflement, these
almost tender hands that once
swung hammers and drove machines
and insisted that I learn to be a man.

The Visitors

Far off down the hill by our house,
my wife is calling my name.
There are visitors, a boy and a man,
both turned my way, shading
their eyes with their hands. I can't
believe the man is my stepfather,
long dead, yet he walks toward me
with the same step, too wide
and deep for his height, inspiring
the old dread. When he reaches
the grave site where I stand, I can see
in his eyes that he remembers
how hard he once worked his stepsons,
and that he would be sorry for it
except it is all part of the earthly
confusion he has left behind.
I understand even in my dream this
is the beginning of my forgiveness,
which he must secure to continue
with the religious work he has been
given for his eternity. Then
I notice the one he has chosen
to accompany him forever, the boy
with patches on his knees who leans
against his shovel, rapt and lost.

An Executive's Afterlife

The others in hell can't believe he's allowed
to go free for eternity. Part of their punishment
as they sit beside the fire in chains is to watch him
pass by. His punishment, after a life of having all
the answers, is to have none whatsoever and keep
bumping into people who ask him questions:
his wife, for instance, here because she never dared
ask him any, choosing to die a slow death instead.
How are you? is all she has to say to make him turn,
always for the first time, to discover her with no
coiffure and ashes on her face. Under his hand,
which never leaves his chest, the pain feels like
the beginnings of the coronary that killed him,
and it only gets worse when he sees the son he bullied,
an old man in chains. Unable to leave the comfort
of his father's wealth and live his own life, rich
or poor, the son now kneels at the flames trying
to get warm, with no result, forever. He's too intent
to ask his question, which the father, on his way,
already knows: *Why did you do this?* Soon he walks
past former doormen, bellhops, and bag ladies
who can't wait to ask him the one thing that makes
their day, even in hell: *Who do you think you are?*
Nobody's nice, except the stewardess from first-class.
She liked serving passengers with expensive suits
and wristwatches so much, she must seek them out
with her eternally nice smile to inquire, *Would you*

like something to drink? She has no drinks,
of course, this is hell, after all, so he's left to suffer
his unquenchable thirst, not a hurt or absence
he feels in the throat, but there under his hand,
in his sensitive and innocent heart, which the devil,
to give him his due, went nearly to heaven to find.

Smoking

Once, when cigarettes meant pleasure
instead of death, before Bogart
got lung cancer and Bacall's
voice, called "smoky," fell

into gravel of a lower octave,
people went to the movies just
to watch the two of them smoke.
Life was nothing but a job,

Bogart's face told us, expressionless
except for the recurrent grimace,
then it lit up with the fire
he held in his hand and breathed

into himself with pure enjoyment
until each word he spoke afterward
had its own tail of smoke.
When he offered a cigarette

to Bacall, she looked right at him,
took it into her elegant mouth
and inhaled, while its smoke curled
and tangled with his. After the show,

just to let their hearts race and taste
what they'd seen for themselves,
the audiences felt in purses,
shirt pockets, and even inside

the sleeves of T-shirts, where packs
of cigarettes were folded, by a method
now largely forgotten. "Got a light?"
somebody would say, "Could I bum

one of yours?" never thinking
that two of the questions most
asked by Americans everywhere
would undo themselves and disappear

like the smoke that rose
between their upturned fingers,
unwanted in a new nation
of smoke-free movie theaters,

malls and restaurants, where politicians
in every state take moral positions
against cigarettes so they can tax them
for their favorite projects. Just fifty years

after Bogart and Bacall, smoking
is mostly left in the hands of waitresses
huddled outside fancy inns, or old
clerks on the night shift in mini-marts,

or hard-hats from the road crew
on a coffee break around the battered
tailgate of a sand truck — all paying
on installment with every drag

for bridges and schools. Yet who else
but these, who understand tomorrow
is only more debt, and know
better than Bogart that life is work,

should be trusted with this pleasure
of the tingling breath they take today,
these cigarettes they bum and fondle,
calling them affectionate names

like "weeds" and "cancer sticks," holding
smoke and fire between their fingers
more casually than Humphrey Bogart
and blowing it into death's eye.

Home

Driving North in Winter

All the way to Mercer these
rooms left out
in the dark —

lamplight and two chairs
the old couple sit
reading in,

a table where a family
comes together
for dinner —

the rest of the houses, one
with the night. How
blessed they are,

the man hanging his ordinary
coat in the small world
of a kitchen,

the woman turning to her cupboard,
both of them held
from the cold

and the vastness by nothing
but trusting
inattention

and one beam of light,
like us passing by
in the darkness,

you napping, me wide awake
and grateful for this
moment

we've also been given, apart
in our way of being
together, living

in the light.

What They Are

Not the four wheels,
but clusters of four
and six wheels spinning
into steel hollows
far below the cab. Not a cab,
but high, dark windows
under a crown of lights
and a vast grille displaying
its name: Papa Bear,
Snow Man, Silver Eagle.
Not a truck, but a bird
lifting up over the hill
outside Rumford with a long,
straight tail of logs,
or in the north woods
a ship drifting down, its tarp
swelling in the rain and wind.
Not a ship, but a starship
landing on the night streets
of Presque Isle, lights in the doors
and all along the roof.
Not a roof, but a bed
for lime from Thomaston,
or a cement mixer slowly
turning, or a sleek vessel
for milk from Kennebec
Valley farms. Not one, not once,

but many, day after day,
passing above us
like great Buddhas
with headlights in their knees
and small hands resting
at their windshields
on roads all over Maine.

Charles by Accident

Named Charlie for the relaxed
companionship we expected,
he became Charles for his butler-like
obedience, though he went off-duty

the morning my wife walked back
from the mailbox watching him
toss what looked like a red sock
gloriously into the air,

seeing it was actually the cardinal
she had been feeding all winter.
Why did she scream like that
was the question his whole,

horrified body seemed to ask, just
before he disappeared, back soon
at the door, black coat, white collar,
all ready to serve us: who was

that other dog, anyway? Who,
on the other hand, was this one,
chosen at the pound for his breed
and small size, now grown into three

or four different kinds of large
dogs stuck together. It wasn't his fault,
of course, that in the end he wasn't
Charlie, or even, considering the way

he barked at guests and sniffed them,
Charles exactly. Besides, it couldn't
have been easy to be whatever
sort of dog he was. Part retriever,

he spent his winters biting ice,
and summers dirt out of his tufted paws.
Part Collie, all he ever got to herd
were two faux sheep: a wire-haired terrier

that bit him back and a cat that turned
and ran up trees. An accidental sheep-dog,
Charles by accident, and our dog only
after he'd been disowned, he understood

that life is all missed connections
and Plan B — the reason why, perhaps,
no one could quite pat him or say
good boy enough, and why sometimes,

asleep, he mourned, working his legs
as if running to a place he could never
reach, beyond Charles or any other
way we could think of to call him.

Town Limits

1

How shy she became when she saw them
outside her kitchen window — her young,
married sister leading the minister's wife
straight up the front walk. How the two
of them, noticing steam over the dishpan,
called and called. How embarrassed
she was when they opened the pantry door
at last and found her, looking up at them
beside her dog, unable to still her heart.

2

The substitute, far off
at the pulpit, asks who
is new today in church,
then raises his hand.
Nobody laughs. It is his voice
that dazes them, a breezy
lighthearted tone for a joke,
an earnest tone for sympathizing
with their need, a helpless
tone for asking God
to assist them. Up close
after the service as they shake
his hand and look into
his evasive eye, they see

the voice is how
he protects himself from them.

3

"A man's property," was what he called his three-
acre lot when they complained about the mess,
and he placed one of his junk machines next
to the road where he said neighbors were driving
on his lawn. There were just ten years of cutting
down trees, and dragging a rusty harrow
over the roots, and skinning off topsoil from the hill
to build up the yard, before the house went quiet
and the rumors started. When they saw him
at town meeting, pale, and skinnier than ever,
even his neighbors felt sorry to see the new
look in his eye which said he had no anger left
about being a have-not: that he never owned a thing.

4

If this was all
there was to winning
the old farmer's praise,
the boy didn't mind
taking up the grain bag
by the barn post.
It wasn't heavy,
and the newborn kittens
hardly made a sound
as he swung it

and swung it, then
laid it down still
between them, not knowing
he would never let it go.

5

"Pink, and here in the bedroom,
of all places," the new owners say
to guests touring their house,
"the plumbing coming up through
these beautiful wide-board floors,"

where now there is no trace of the toilet
old Frank put in beside Bernice,
who was by then too sick to get up
from her bed and use the flush
she'd always dreamed of, and woke

sometimes thinking it was a dream,
this seat above a bowl of water
you could release with a small, delicate
handle, right indoors, and called Frank
to make him do it, and said it was beautiful.

6

When he spoke to neighbors
and friends, casual in his authority,
the wife mostly listened.
"You left out the important part,"
she would say, while he

brushed her aside and went on.
"But that time you took the car
to Canada, I was there with you."

When they talked about their dogs,
male and female terriers, she
was in charge of the conversation.
"Sometimes she actually
bites him for ignoring her.
You should see him follow her
around then. He sleeps with his head
touching hers, all night long."

    7

The trouble with Hunts is
that when they tell about
what somebody did
to somebody else you never
know if the somebody did it
or if the other somebody
or somebody else
entirely did it
or should have done it
or would have, though what it
was whoever it was did it
was only something like it
really was or might have been,
or nothing at all like it,
or just nothing, nothing at all.

8

It's not so amazing that Francis
has used his eighty-four-year-
old lungs all morning
to blow a saxophone

with old Cunliffe on the bagpipes,
or that stopping his car
to lean out the window and talk
he hardly strains the seat belt

his dog ate most of,
or that underneath
its skinny band
he's wearing a Florida shirt

he got out of the clothes closet
in his old house across the road
from the new house he moved into
twelve years back; what's amazing

is his ability to tell you all
about it in give or take one minute,
including three or four pauses
with yups and a good-bye wave.

Home

Under bands of light
in the long hall, the old
woman walks, her face

bright as if she knows
where she is going
and dull again and bright

and dull again; she turns
and walks the other way.
The man in #203 stands

in the back field
all afternoon calling
the hired man. Johnson

is also the name of the one
in the wheelchair
though he would not

respond to it, now reduced
to the question
on his face: What

happened to me?
Near him in the lobby,
squinting, Do I Know You

leans forward, and beside her,
face fastened
to an oxygen tube,

I'm Scared. They don't
raise their eyes to the TV,
jumping with its

fake life. Three times
a day they hold
their forks and do not

eat their food. And when
the family arrives, tourists
from a country they'll never

see again, they can't think how
they have ended up
in the home

where they are all
homeless, or why
they are waving back

to those they hardly recall,
or why their visitors
are smiling.

Shovels

Who could have guessed he would choose
to spend so much of his time bent over
a shovel, one wrist so weak he wore
an ace bandage on it, his asthmatic lungs
forcing him to stop for breath again
and again. "Never mind," he would say to us,
his three young stepsons, when we stopped,
too, "get back to work."
                            Every weekend
for a whole winter, we hauled cinders
from the paper mill to level the driveway.
That next spring he had us digging holes
for the barn's corner posts, angry that we kept
fighting with one another in our anger
about the endlessness of banging our shovels
into the nearly frozen ground. Why did he
drive us that way? Why was he so hard
on himself, always the last one to come
in the house out of the dark?
                            One summer
we dug until we found ourselves inside
a waist-high trench he said would bring water
up from the river to the plants of his nursery.
"You'll never get anywhere," he told us,
"until you learn the meaning of work."

Above ground in the moonlight, as I return
through this poem, the tall grass has no idea
where we laid that pipe. The sprinkler system
for the nursery, dead for years, has forgotten why.
All the truckloads of fill we brought to prevent
the bank's erosion are on their way down
into the river. In the back of the old barn,
its aluminum siding curled from the weather,
the shovels we once used stand upside-down
against the wall in the window's light like flowers,
making a kind of memorial to the work
we did then, some with blunted points, some
scalloped at the center, where after all those years
of shoveling, they shoveled themselves away.

The Good-Boy Suit

I was four when my mother
stitched herself, working late
at night, my father gone.
She put her hand into the light

of the Singer and pressed
the treadle until the needle
sang through her thumb.
I stood back from the piles

of clothes she sewed afterward
with her bandaged hand,
fingers flashing under her shut
face, gone away herself.

She would not stitch me,
I thought. But I was a bad boy,
and why did my mother say over
and over she would sew me

a new suit if I was good?
I was afraid to be good,
I was afraid not to be good.
My mother switched me.

My mother switched and stitched.
Turn around, she said, pushing pins
with her bandage into the patterns
on my arms and chest, Stand still,

making a tickle when she measured
my inseam. I was the bad boy
who couldn't, who forgot
to flush, who was afraid

to clean out from under the bed
or watch my mother lean
forward putting her hand into
the Singer's light that was like fire

in her eyes and hair.
The good-boy suit just let her
stick pins in it and cut it
and push it into the fire again

and again with her shut face
to stitch it, only the two of them
together in the dark all night long.
So when I came downstairs

to find them, my mother
held up the good-boy suit
that had my arms and chest
and legs. It's perfect, she said,

smiling at it, and her hand, with no
bandage now, was perfect too.
I was the one who wasn't.
I couldn't answer when my mother

asked me why I did not like
or want the good-boy suit,
or why, even at a time like this,
I had to be such a bad boy.